A Love Letter For Loretta
An Indiana Murder Case, Solved

A Love Letter For Loretta
    An Indiana Murder Case, Solved

For Lert.
May you rest in peace now.

Although this book is based on a true story, certain names and time frames have been changed for issues of respect and privacy.

ONE / September, 1974

Her name was Loretta.

I didn't know her well – actually, I only knew her a very brief period of time – but in the end, I'd felt as though I'd known her for a lifetime.

And to think it had all begun with another one of my drunken binges and severe hangovers.

#

I had been sitting at my old battered typewriter, working on yet another "great American novel" when I'd suddenly been hit with a severe case of the dreaded writer's block.

Normally, I would just pop a cold beer, sip a little single malt, and my clouded brain would loosen up. But that day, I had been lucky just to remember to tie my shoes.

But, ever the determined drunk, I'd decide to take a short break, walk down to the neighborhood watering hole, and allow the general atmosphere to unlock my booze soaked brain cells.

As it turned out, I needn't have worried about it; and angel unlocked it for me.

#

Her name was Loretta.

An attractive, petite blond with a warm smile and a winning personality, she had captured my attention as soon as I walked into the tavern.

She had been standing by the ancient jukebox feeding it coin after coin, paying a wide variety of different types of music – easy listening, pop, and country tunes mostly – and sipping a mug of beer.

Suddenly, it was as though we are the only two people in the place, my attentions focused mainly on her and her wiley charms.

She noticed I was staring at her – couldn't help myself, to be honest – and she sauntered over to me at the bar, wearing a big smile that would have melted even the coldest of hearts, and said, "I haven't seen you in here before. My name is Loretta."

Speechless at first – awestruck by her natural beauty – I managed to say, "My name is Chuck."

She sat down at a nearby table, and said, "So, Chuck, what do you do for a living? You don't seem like the type to be working long hours at the steel mill."

This lady is very perseptive, I thought, and said, "I am a writer. Well, an "aspiring" writer, that is."

She motioned to me to have a seat at the table with her, which I did, and she said, "What do you write? Newspaper articles and stuff?"

I said, "Well, right now, I'm working on what I hope is going to be the next great American novel."

She said, "Sounds exciting. So...what will the book be about?"

Staring into those beautiful eyes of hers, I lost my focus for a moment, and said, "To be honest? I'm not sure just yet. I guess whatever comes to mind at the time."

She said, "Well, Chuck the aspiring writer, want to play a game of pool?"

I said, "A woman after my own heart. Sure. Eight ball to start?"

She smiled and said, "Eight ball it is. I'll rack them."

As I stood watching her rack the cueballs, I couldn't help but notice that suddenly, all eyes in the place were now focused on us.

The bartender, and most of the other bar patrons, were all watching us intently, as though they'd never seen two people playing pool before. One man, a tall, lanky fella with deep set, dark eyes like a doll's eyes, stood close by, sipping beer from a can and watching us like a hawk.

As we began playing pool, I whisperd to her, "You know the guy giving us the eyeball? He is getting on my nerves."

Glancing around briefly, she grinned and said, "Oh, that's just Lee. He's a regular. He is harmless, though, don't pay him any mind."

I said, "If he doesn't stop staring at me pretty soon, I'm going to show how *harmless* I am, too."

She said, "Don't pay him any mind. Let's just shoot pool, okay?"

Helpless to argue with those eyes and smile, I said, "Okay, pretty lady. Let's play pool."

#

As the night went on, and we played several more games of pool, Loretta had apparently grown tired of my paranoia over Lee, and had eventually lost interest, taking off to mingle with the rest of her friends, and left me to my own paranoia and sucking down fifty-cent draft beers.

I too, rapidly grew tired of paranoid stares and lukewarm beer, and had left for home, deciding that my little cramped apartment and my ancient typewriter seemed more appealing at the time.

Little did I know at the time, our brief encounter at the local tavern would end up changing my life forever.

TWO

I'd gone home that night and ended up typing up about four pages, which for me at the time, was a real accomplishment.

By around midnight, my brain soaked in booze and my stomach growling like a bear, I had eaten a Hungryman TV dinner, then I'd gone to bed early, and thankfully slept like a baby.

The next day, though, sleep had been the furthest thing from my mind.

#

By the time I'd done the shit, shower, and shave routine, and popped my first beer of the day, I was feeling my oats again, and had sat down to work on the book.

I wasn't sure where I was going with the book, but I'd find out soon enough,

About an hour later, the local newspaper arrived at my door, and on the front page, in big, bold block letters the headlines read:

Local Woman Reported Missing From Tavern

As I read the article, I realized it was Loretta.

I was literally stunned by what I was reading; I was with her just last night, playing pool and having a grand old time. Now, this mysterious, lovely lady was missing. Foul play was suspected, too.

I sipped some scotch now, some single malt, to calm my nerves. It didn't help much.

So I sipped some more.

#

Later that day, as I sat on the front porch of my apartment building, chatting with one of the other tenants about the newspaper article – he said he thought it was most likely aliens that took her, then again, his idea of good literature was reading the *National Enquirer* – I glanced up to see an ummarked patrol car pull up.

I knew by reading one of my favorite magazines, *True Detective*, that only Detectives drove unmarked cars. Sure enough, a tall, lanky fella wearing a suit with a gold badge on his belt climbed out of the Sedan, and walked up to us and he said, matter-of-factly, "Good afternoon, gentlemen. Do either of you know where I can find a fellow named Chuck Polanski?"

I said, "What do you want to talk to him about? I hear he's pretty busy these days."

He lit a cigarette and said, "That's between me and him, friend. Now, do you know where I can find him?"

I stood up and said, "I'm Chuck Polaski, sir, and I am sorta busy right now."

He grinned and said, "Yes, I can see how busy you are. But could you spare a few minutes? It is really important."

For some reason, I knew he wanted to talk about

Loretta, so I said, "Is this about the lady that disappeared from the tavern last night?"

He said, "What makes you say that?"

I said, "Because I'm not stupid, that's why."

He said, "Fair enough. May we talk in private? It will only take a few minutes."

I said, "Okay, but I'm telling you up front, I don't have any idea what happened to her."

He said, "We'll see. May we go inside?"

#

Once inside my apartment, as I popped a beer and sat down at the kitchen table, he sat down across from me and didn't waste any time getting down to business.

Lighting another Pall Mall non filter, he said, "So, Mr Polanski, tell me about last night."

I said, "There's not much to tell, really. I got bored sitting at my typewriter, and walked down to the tavern to have a beer or two."

He said, "You're a writer, are you?"

I said, "*Aspiring* writer, yes."

He said, "What do you write about?"

I said, "Whatever comes to mind. I am very opinionated at times, too."

The detective grinned at me and said, "I bet you are, Mr Polanksi."

I said, "Meaning?"

He said, "Most writers are opinionated aren't they? That's how they make money."

Growing tired of his little game, I said, "If you have something to ask me, just do it. I've got single malt to drink and a story to write."

Cracking that big, shit eating grin of his again, he said, "Fair enough. Did you have anything to do with this woman's disappearance, Mr Polanksi? Not that it matters that much."

A woman's life doesn't matter much? I thought. What an asshole. I said, "No, I did not. We played pool for a while, drank some beer, and I came home."

He said, "Did you see anyone else paying attention to her? I mean, anyone that could be considered the suspicious type?"

I said, "There was one guy, she said his name was Lee, kept staring me down. But she said he was harmless."

He said, "Yes, I've already spoken with him, and he is no longer a suspect."

I said, "So, am I a suspect?"

He said, "I'm usually a pretty good judge of character, and to be honest, you don't seem like the type to kidnap anyone. Then again, looks can be decieving."

I said, "Well, Mr?"

He said, "Detective Lester Manly."

I said, "Well, Mr Manly, I don't rightly give a hair on the crack of a rat's ass what you think of me. Secondly, like I said, I'm busy. Is there anything else you want to ask me?"

He put his cigarette out in the ashtray, stood to his feet, and said, "For now, no. But you never know when I might drop by again for a chat."

I stood up and said, "I can't wait."

He grinned again, turned around and left, without another word. I just stood there for a few moments, trying to keep my temper under control, so I wouldn't be tempted to follow him outside and shove his shiny gold badge up his ass.

Then I popped another beer, sat down at my typewriter, and began writing again.

Little did I know at the time, my next story would span almost forty years.

THREE / Summer, 2014

Over a span of forty years, I'd been through a lot of shit.

Drug addiction, alcoholism, jail. Homelessness, hunger and more alcoholism. Dead end jobs that never lasted long.

Looking back, I'm really surprised that I made it to early retirement age, but I'm glad I did.

I now had all the time in the world to conduct my own little "investigation" into what happened to Loretta.

I never forgot about her.

#

For almost forty years, no matter how my own sad, excuse for a life was going, she was always in the back of my mind, like a headache that wouldn't go away.

A pretty, mysterious, pleasant headache, yes, but a void in my brain that would never be filled unless I solved the case, regardless of risk to life and limb.

I'd spent a lot of my spare time over th last ten years or so, with the age of the internet now in full swing, to utilize the vast, world wide web to my advantage.

I must admit, modern technology, by 2014, was amazing.

And...very informative.

It hadn't taken me long to find a few articles on

Loretta's disappearance – and subsequent death.

As I sat there that day, reading over the articles, I broke down in tears from time to time, doing my best to block out what the last few hours of her life would have been like for her.

She had apparently been abducted from the tavern parking lot, taken somewhere else, strangled to death, and dumped in a cornfield like a piece of trash.

The testimonies her surviving family members gave to the media were equally as heart wrenching.

Her niece, Gayle, told me the following heartbreaking story after visiting the murder site:

I remember going over to the cornfield you could see the outline of her body, pieces of her hair was in the mud, her finger nails where laying there , little pieces of her skirt was in the mud. She had laid there in muddy water for a while and they said the animals and the birds had got to her. It was horrible. Was she killed here and then dumped over there? WHY wasn't anyone trying to help us find out what happened?

Very good question.

Ann, Loretta's eldest daughter, had this to say:

When Mom first went missing, my dad and my brothers went everywhere to look for her, if any one thought they saw her. it didn't matter where, they would go, this went on the entire time she was missing. It was always a big let down when they would return from a sighting and didn't have any news, We always felt like the police were not doing anything and we all felt helpless. The not knowing was so hard, always wondering if she was hurt some where and couldn't get help or if she was being held against her will, the thoughts you have are horrible. None of us really knew what to do. But we all KNEW something was wrong.

Something was wrong, indeed.

Something horribly wrong.\

Yes, I had my work cut out for me, that's for sure – but I never gave up.

FOUR

I had put aside all of my other literary projects for the time being, and concentrated primarily on the murder case.

Besides, what else would I be doing otherwise? Getting sloppy drunk and making a fool of myself? Passing out in a puddle of my own puke?

Yes, Loretta's murder case was a very welcome distraction to say the least.

Not to say that I had *stopped* drinking, mind you. Me not drinking on a daily basis, would have been like me signing my own death certificate. I had tried drying out in the past, and my whole body had begun to betray me, so sick I almost ended up in the hospital.

Point being, a full fledged, dedicated drunk whose body has become *dependent* on alcohol, cannot simply "dry out," so to speak. Your body will rebel against such an action, and will most likely *kill* you.

But at least I cared enough about solving this case, when it seemed like nobody else – those in positions of authority – even gave a damn.

I'm no hero by a long shot, mind you, but I'm not a quitter, either.

#

I started out by doing more research into the guy at the bar that day, that kept staring me down.

Lee.

Come to find out, his full name was Lee Underhill, Jr. - a man with a very colorful past.

Over the last twenty years or so, he had been arrested – and convicted – of being a child molester. He was not only an overbearing, loud mouthed, drunken womanizer, but a pedophile as well.

The more I looked into the case, the more I understood why he was staring me down that day; he had his eye set on Loretta, and I was in his way.

He had been *jealous* of my presence there, and wanted me out of the way.

Unforunately, for Loretta, I'd gone home early, and left her wide open and vulnerable to his nefarious intentions.

I had begun to feel like it was *my* fault she had been murdered.

Believe me, that's *not* a good feeling.

So...on with the case I go.

FIVE

It may sound odd, but at times, I believe that women were *born* to suffer.

How else could you explain why so many women are willing to do almost anything, even for the smallest declaration of love?

I hope I'm wrong; too many innocent women have perished already.

#

With those unpleasant thoughts rolling in my head, I popped another beer, took a shot of single malt, and sat down at my laptop to do some more research into Mr Underhill.

What I found out was less than positive.

He had *died* many years ago, and would no longer be available for any questioning, arrest, or conviction.

I'd felt like a piece of my heart had died that day, too.

So, as usual, whenever I had experienced a big disappointment, I had gotten drunker than a barrel full of retarded monkeys.

I woke up on the kitchen floor, a day and half later, in a puddle of my own piss.

Like father, like worthless son.

#

I woke up cold, dizzy, nauseated, and had a large cigarette burn on my right thigh. To add insult to injury, I had also lost control of my bladder during the blackout, and I'm lying in a pool of my own urine.

I finally manage to get up off the floor, my head filled with visions of my past, flashing through my mind like a VHS tape on fast-forward.

I sees my parents – both now deceased – in a happier time, both much younger and full of life. I see my cat, Toby, my childhood pet, scampering to meet me as I exit the school bus. He was struck by a car when I was nine years old, leaving me heartbroken for months. I felt so alone after his death, being an only child.

I block these images from my mind, take a long cold shower, pop a beer, take a shot of single malt, and sit down at the computer again.

Some hero for Loretta to depend on, huh?

#

As I sat at the computer, surfing the internet for more info on the Underhill family, I suddenly come upon the obituary for Lee, and his funeral proceedings.

Something I should have thought of before.

A list of the attendees – which wasn't many – some of which would be his surviving family members.

Bingo!

I write down several names, and conduct a search for them as well.

To my utter surprise, one of his surviving family

members is one of my *neighbors*.

So, I log into Facebook to conduct another search for the neighbor.

It's amazing, really, how the age of the internet has made it so easy to find someone. That could be a curse, too, depending on your past.

I would hate to see what people could dig up on yours truly. They would find that their Facebook friend or drinking buddy was one of the worst, troublesome, hardcore sons of bitches that ever strolled the streets of this quaint little town.

But for now, I must concentrate on my neighbor.

SIX

It hadn't taken long to find what I was looking for.

She had her whole family history listed with her Facebook account, which wasn't too smart on her part, but was an advantage for me.

As it turned out, Mr rapist murderer was her own grandfather, which I'm quite sure she hadn't told anyone. That is, if she even knew the truth about him at all.

I doubt her mother had bragged about him too much.

So...I had decided to befriend her on Facebook, and see what I could come up with through casual conversation. As it turned out, this lady was smart enough to see right through me, through my primary goal in chatting with her, and she blocked me.

But, never one to give up easily, I stuck to my guns and carried on, and what I found out was much more relevant than anything she might have lied about.

#

The whole case, in itself, was a total clusterfuck of different roads to travel.

For example, the smartass detective that had questioned me so many years ago, had shown no more interest in the case than was needed. Apparently, in his opinion, Loretta – and the other members of her family

– were nothing more than North End trash, and he wasn't about to spend any more time than he had to in solving it.

Good riddance to bad rubbish, in his personal opinion.

So, it was up to someone else to pick up the pieces, and that person was yours truly.

And what a wild ride it turned out to be.

#

To my surprise – and disappointment – Mr Lester Manley had died too, so I couldn't question him, either, and not that it would have done any good to do so. He probably would have lied about his own shortcomings, if he had been willing to speak with me at all.

Strike three.

But, I wasn't going to give up just yet.

Yes, Lee was dead.

Yes, so was Detective smartass.

And yes, his granddaughter would not speak to me about the case.

But, nobody concerned knew who they would be messing with, either. I am a drunk, yes, but I am also a very *determined* drunk when I set my mind to it.

If that makes any sense.

If not, you can kiss my ass. Unless you've walked a mile in my shoes, don't be the first one in line to cast judgement.

So, onward I go.

SEVEN

Onward to what, exactly, I wasn't quite sure of just yet.

But I'd find out soon enough.

Once I start digging, I am like a bloodhound sniffing out a fox.

I may drink too much, but in all honesty, I consider it one of my strengths. Deep down, I know that I have to pay *special attention* to everything I do, as not to screw up my life anymore than it is already screwed up. That may sound crazy to some folks, but it has always worked out for me in the end.

The next day, after I'd worked up the gumption to clean up the big piss stain in my kitchen, I'd sat back down at my computer for some more research.

After several more hours of fruitless searching, I had come to the sad conclusion that if I was going to prove that the late Lee Underhill Jr. was guilty of murder, have it on record, providing Loretta's surviving family members with any sense of closure, it as going to be a long, hard road to any type of success.

Then again, there is actually no such thing as *real* closure.

Closure is a *word*, and that's about the extent of it.

In reality, the only form of "closure" anybody ever experiences is the fatc that they know who did something awful, and why.

But otherwise?

The surviving family members are stuck living their own life sentence forever, the memory of what happened to their loved one always eating away at them, like a cancer.

Closure is actually the act of learning to live with the memories, making a place for it in your heart, then moving on.

Believe me, I know this from experience.

#

Feeling as though I was now between a rock and a hard place, I'd decided to make one, last pitch effort at speaking with Underhill's grandaughter.

I had been blocked on Facebook, so I had resorted to sneaking down to her place after dark, and leaving a note in her mailbox.

To my utter surprise, I woke up the next day to find a note in my mailbox, from her, letting me know that if I wanted to speak to her about the case, there were to be two conditions.

Number one, we'd meet up in a public place.

Number two, her name was *not* to be included in my story.

I readily agreed, amd hoped for the best.

As it turned out, my inquiry had been in vain.

EIGHT

We had agreed to meet up at a local park nearby.

At one time, it had been a safe haven for the neighborhood kids to hang out, but over the years, just like all other safe havens, it had eventually become a hang out for the criminals.

Keeping this in mind, I had stuffed my .22 caliber revolver down the back of my pants before heading out to the park.

Better to be safe than sorry.

#

As I sat at one of the old picnic tables, reading over the graffiti that had scrawled there over the years, I heard a voice coming from behind me.

A shy, timid voice, like a child.

I turned around to see a short, stocky woman with a baby face, her general appearance totally void of any sign she had to be in her fifties by now.

She said, "Are you Mr Polanski?"

I stood to my feet, extending my hand, and said, "Yes ma'am. And you are Miss Melinda Handler?"

She shook my hand, and dropped it like it burnt her skin, and said, "Yes. Can we go ahead and get this over with? I work third shift tonight."

"Of course," I said, sitting down. She did the

same, and said, "So, what is it exactly you want to know?"

I lit a cigarette, offered her one, and she turned it down. I said, "Well, first of all, how well did you know your grandfather?"

She said, "Not very well, actually. He was in prison when I was a little girl, so I didn't really have a chance to know him back then."

I said, "Why was he in prison, if I may ask?"

She said, embarrassingly, "I'd rather not discuss the details, if it's okay with you."

I said, "Of course, I'm sorry."

She said, "No reason for an apology. You had no way of knowing."

I said, "Thank you. Now, I know this may be hard for you to hear, but, I believe your grandfather was involved in the disppearance – and death – of a local woman back in the seventies."

She squirmed around nervously, and said, "Yes, I have heard all about it, from my mother."

I said, "What did she tell you, if I may ask?"

Squirming around again, her face flushed with embarrassment, she said, "Not much, except for the fact he was questioned by the police in her death. A lot of other folks were too, but none of it panned out."

Lighting another cigarette, I said, "What do *you* think happened? From an observer's point of view?"

She said, "Honestly? I'm not sure what to think, after his so called death bed confession."

Bingo! I thought, but did my best to hide my excitement from her.

I said, calmly, "So, what did he say, if I may ask?"

Her hands were trembling as she said, "He said *he*

was the one who had killed her. That it was an accident, because he was so drunk."

I said, "What do *you* think?"

She said, "I don't know what to think, honestly. I wasn't there, my mother told me what he said."

I said, "*When* did she tell you?"

She said, "Not until many years later. She thought if I was an adult, it would more easy to handle the truth."

I said, "And was it easier?"

She hung her head and said, "Not really, no. It;s been eating away at me all these years, like a cancer. That's why I decided to speak with you after all."

I said, "And I appreciate that. May I ask you one more question before you go?"

Glancing at her wristwatch, she said, "Sure, if you make it quick."

I said, "Fair enough. My question is, do you know of any evidence that might be available for me to look at? Any old court records, autopsy reports, anything that might help me write my story?"

She said, "I'm sorry, Mr Polanski, but I don't know of anything like that. I'm quite sure my parents wouldn't have kept it around, anyway. The bad memories, the embarrassment of it all, you know?"

I said, "Of course, I'm sorry."

Standing up, she said, "Well, I better get going, I have a long shift ahead of me tonight."

I stood to my feet and said, "Thank you again for speaking with me. I know it must have been hard on you."

She forced a smile and said, "It's okay, Mr Polanski, I've done a lot of difficult things in my life, and I'm still here."

As she turned to leave, I said, "Miss Handler?"

She stopped and said, "Yes?"

I said, "One more thing; why did *you* wait so long to come forward with this story?"

Turning her steely gaze away from me, she said, as she walked away, "*Goodbye*, Mr Polanksi."

I never saw her or heard from her again after that day. After thinking it over, I guess it was for the best.

Now, it was time to move on again.

I had other people to talk to.

But first, I needed a drink.

NINE

That night, as I sat nursing a glass of scotch and watching reruns of *Cops*, I tried to relax, but the conversation I'd had with Melinda was still weighing heavily on my mind.

Not only had our chat been less than informative, but kind of fishy as well.

I may not have a college degree or a high IQ, but what I do have is *street smarts*. Believe me when I tell you, street smarts come in really handy when you are journeying into places your average Joe would not dare to venture.

Therefore, I know when I'm being fed a line of bullshit, and I was definitely less than satisfied with our conversation.

But, for now, time to move forward again, and rely on my wits to get me through.

#

But, first things first.

I had read on line that since Loretta's body had been found in Illinois, it was the Lawrence County, Illinois coroner I'd have to speak to about any autopsy reports.

The whole case, from the very beginning, had been so hush-hush up until now, I couldn't help but wonder if the Illinois county coroner might have some useful information.

So, the next day, I looked up the phone number, and gave him a call.

Problem was, he was dead now, too.

The presiding coroner was less than friendly, or helpful either one. When I was asked what case I was looking into, there was dead silence on the other end of the line, followed by a pre-recorded, robotic voice informing me I was being placed on hold, and to be patient.

After waiting for around eight minutes, I suddenly heard a human voice on the line.

"Interim coroner Jesse Davis. How may I help you, Mr Polanski?"

I said, "Well, I'm currently looking into an old case, a murder case, from the year nineteen-seventy-four."

She said, "Oh my, everything in our records department has been digitalized now. A case that old may not even be in our system."

I said, adamantly, "Well, would you please take a look for me anyway? It's really important to the surviving family members."

With an audible sigh of exasperation, she said, "Alright, Mr Polanksi, give me few moments."

Before I could reply, the line went dead for a second or two, and some of what I refer to as "elevator music" began playing in the background. Sighing with exasperation myself, I just leaned back in my desk chair and waited impatiently.

Several minutes later, Jesse was back, clearing her throat before she said, "Well, Mr Polanksi, I'm sorry, but all we have left of those records are some old paper copies, and they look as though they have been water damaged, possibly from a water leak."

Sighing again, I said, "That's fine. Can you mail them to me? I don't drive right now, and I live in Indiana."

She sighed again and said, "Sure, Mr Polanski. I'll send them out with tomorrow's mail."

After giving her my postal address, she hung up without so much as goodbye or kiss my ass, and I felt the same way, wishing I could have hung up on her instead.

It was three weeks before I recieved the paper copies in the mail, and it looked like this:

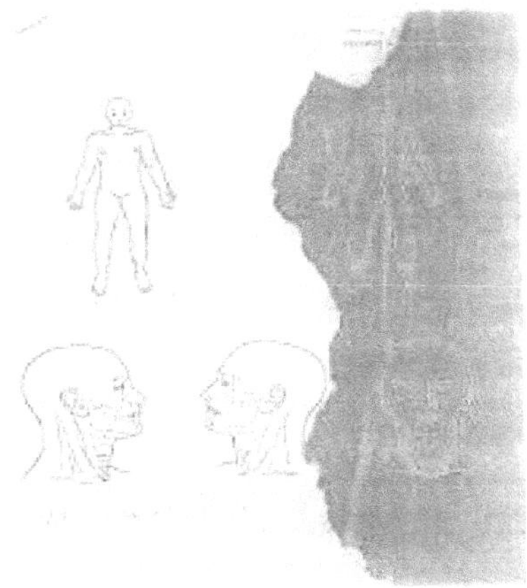

Needless to say, I wasn't very happy with the results of my inquiry.

But, it's all I had for now, so as usual, I moved forward, keeping my fingers crossed.

But first, I had a drink.

Gotta have some inspiration, you know?

TEN

The next morning, after my usual shit shower and shave routine – and a couple of cold beers, I went back to work on the case.

For what it was worth.

I was already beginning to lose hope in solving the case, and that wasn't in my nature. All of my life, good times or bad, I had always managed to muddle through each difficult situation, whether it turned out good or bad.

But...this was different.

This time, I had absolutely nothing to work with, running into another obstacle at every turn.

So, I did what I would normally do in times of being stuck in dire straits; I got drunk.

#

But this time, I ended up in worse shape than I'd been in years.

This time, I had gone into a blackout state, and lost three days, and where they went to, I still can't tell you to this day.

Blackouts are terrible to say the least.

You are totally awake, yet you aren't aware of anything you are doing. That is, unless you are sipping from the bottle again, and then your mind seems to be as clear as a mountain stream.

Blackouts can even cause dementia, which can lead to permanent brain damage, and even death.

That is, right before you faint dead away.

Before fainting, you may have sweaty palms, dizziness, trouble seeing, and nausea. After that, the *real* fun begins.

When I woke up from that last blackout, I found myself in the bathrooom floor, lying in front the toilet, buck naked, my chin and chest smeared with vomit, and unable to even breathe, until I threw up again.

My head was reeling and my stomach tied up in knots, and my throat was so raw from throwing up, it was bleeding from the dry heaves.

But, I made it.

This time.

#

The next morning, after I'd had some more sleep and taken a long hot shower, I'd sat at the kitchen table, nursing a cold beer, and contemplating what I was going to do next.

About the case, that is.

I knew, deep down in my heart, that I had a terrible drinking problem – had most of my adult life – and unless I began trying to solve this case in at least a somewhat sober fashion, I would most definitely fail in my next attempt, and let her family down in the process.

What I really needed deep down, was some sense of redemption.

Forgiveness.

From God.

Could solving this case redeem me for my past sins? Maybe, maybe not.

But I had to find out – or die trying.

For Loretta, if not for myself.

One final love letter for Loretta, in the form of her case being laid to rest.

Amen.

ELEVEN

But first, I had to do something that I felt was most likely going to be a bust, but also felt like I had no other choice.

Speak to someone in authority.

Which, in this case, was going to speaking with a local Detective, to see if one of them would help me look up any relelvant info on a forty year old cold case.

Good luck.

#

That afternoon, after settling my nerves with single malt scotch, I'd ventured down to the local cop shop to request a conversation with one of their Detectives, in order to have some much needed assistance in solving the case.

As it turned out, I needn't have bothered.

Upon walking into the main lobby and requesting to speak to a detective, I was met an odd gaze by the lady cop at the front desk, no doubt a reaction to some old fart that reeked of booze requesting a chat with someone who for all I knew might have arrested me for some alcohol related offense in the past.

But she was polite, asked me why, and after I'd told her, picked up her desk phone, pushed a button, whispered something to the other party, hung up, and said, "It will be a few minutes, Mr Polanksi, just have a seat."

I did so, popping a piece of chewing gum in my mouth to mask the odor of scotch, and waited patiently for my chat.

Several minutes later, a tall fella with short cropped hair wearing a Polo shirt and penny loafers walked out and said, "Mr Polanksi? I'm Detective Ed Wagner. I understand you want to talk about a possible cold case?"

I said, matter-of-factly, "It's not a *possible* cold casde, it's a *real* cold case."

Wagner smile and said, "Yes, of course. Follow me."

He lead me to a small office down the hallway, with his name emblazoned on a gold plaque on one of the doors. He opened the door, motioned to me to step inside, and I did so, nervously, and took a seat in front of his desk.

He sat down behind the cluttered desktop, sipped a cup of coffee, and said, "Coffee? It's fresh."

I said, "No thank you. I'm fine."

He leaned back in his chair and said, "So, Mr Polanski. What case is it you want to talk about?"

I placed some printouts on the case I'd found on line about the case on his desk, along with the autopsy report. I said, "This one. It's been cold since nineteen seventy four, despite her family trying to pursue it many times, with no success."

He picked up the printouts and began looking them over, saying, "Hmm...I see."

I said, "I'm glad you see something, because nobody else has. Or, they didn't want to take the time to see something."

He stopped looking at the printouts and said, "What do you mean?"

I said, "The detective that was originally assigned to the case, he could care less, and just allowed it to grow cold."

Wagner said, "Meaning?"

I said, "Just what I said, Mr Wagner. *Nobody* has shown any real interest in this case from the beginning. If it wasn't for me, the case would have been completely forgotten by now."

Wagner said, "I see. So, you really think this case is worth pursuing? I mean, It *is* forty years old now."

I said, "Yes, I definitely believe it is worth pursuing. Her family deserves some peace of mind."

Wagner glanced at the printouts again and said, "It says here, your main suspect died. Exactly how will this provide her family any *real* closure?"

I said, "*Think* about it. Wouldn't you want some type of closure if it was a member of *your* family?"

He sat studying my face for a few moments and said, "Okay, Mr Polanski. I'll give it a shot. I must admit, you've done your homework on this case."

I said, proudly, "Damn right I have."

He said, "Well, Mr Polanski, just leave this information with me, and of course, I'll do some digging of my own. Give me a few days, and I'll get back to you, okay?"

"Thank you," I said, standing to leave. "And my address and other personal info are included with those printouts."

As I turned to leave, Wagner said, "Oh and Mr Polanski, you will have to remember, I can't make any promises on a forty year old case."

I said, "It's okay, Mr Wagner. I'm used to broken promises."

Then I walked out.

#

As I walked home, my mind racing and my nerves shot and my stomach cramping with alcohol withdrawls, I barely made it back to my apartment before I began to heave up my guts all over again.

I stopped and ducked into a nearby alley, voiding my insides of all the leftover impurities, then, after doing my best to compose myself, I staggered the rest of the way home, barely making it through the front door before collapsing on the couch.

I didn't wake up until around midnight.

While I slept, I had another nightmare.

But this time, it was about Loretta.

TWELVE

As soon as I closed my eyes, vivid and horrifying visions of what happened to Loretta plagued my sleep.

It was as if I was really there, watching it all unfold, but was helpless to intervene.

Frozen in time, a statue of cowardice and shame.

As I watched helplessly, I was standing in the parking lot of the Third Base bar, after dark. Close by, I could hear music blaring from the ancient jukebox inside, some sad love song about crying a tear in your beer and watching the love of your life fade away before your eyes.

As I stood frozen, unable to move or speak, I heard the back door to the bar swing open, and out came Loretta, swinging her tiny hips to the beat of the music inside, and smiling like she didn't have a care in the world.

As she stood near the sidewalk, as if she were waiting for someone, the back door burst open, and out came Lee, staggering about on his feet, and spotted Loretta standing close by.

He did an about face, almost falling over, and headed in her direction, saying something I couldn't hear, as though my ears were blocked from any sound now.

At first, whatever he said to her must have been amusing, because she cracked a smile and said something back to him and he smiled as well.

Then, as he began to step closer to her, he said something that must have lacking in humor, because her smile suddenly furrowed into a frown.

As she began yelling at him, using hand gestures to further proclaim her distaste for his sense of humor, he moved closer to her, his fists balled up in anger.

I wanted to scream *Run, Loretta, run!* But my vocal chords were frozen as well.

I tried to move and my feet were frozen to the ground. That's when he made his move.

He lunged toward her, swinging his right fist cruelly into her jaw – I could hear it break on impact – and she went down, limp as a ragdoll, her pretty face striking the pavement.

Just as quickly as he had knocked her to the ground, he snatched her limp body up in his arms, carried her to his truck, yanked open the passenger's side door, and dumped her inside.

Suddenly, thick smoke filled the air around me, choking me, like I was standing behind a huge truck exhaust. I choked, went temporarily blind, and then when the smoke cleared, I was standing in the middle of a corn field, in the dark, alone, as though a time machine had transported me there, and I felt like I was standing in an episode of *The Twilight Zone.*

Dizzy and disoriented, I shook my head to clear it just as I heard the sound of a vehicle approaching in the distance. I rubbed my eyes and looked up to see Lee's old pickup truck coming through the field, mowing down corn stalks and tossing clumps of dirt around like it was confetti.

The truck suddenly came to a halt, billowing

black smoke into the air like a cloud, choking me again and momentarily blinding me.

As the smoke cleared, I could see him yanking open the passenger's side door again, and pulling Loretta's limp body out of the cab, and dumping her on the ground like so much trash.

But this time, she didn't look at all like herself – that is, the *living* version of herself.

Her eyes, once so vivid and full of life, were now like two burnt holes in a blanket, so deeply dark and empty.

Lee stood over her body, like a predator guarding it't kill, lit a cigarette, and proceeded to unzip his pants and urinate in the weeds nearby.

Afterward, he giggled like a school boy, zipped up his pants, and walked to the bed of the truck to retrieve a beer from his cooler. He popped it, drained it, and burped loudly, then, after tossing the empty can next to her body, climbed in his truck, started the engine, and began to leave.

But, not before he stopped, rolled down his window, looked straight at me, and said with an evil grin, *There, Mr Writer. Write a story about THAT.*

That's when I woke up screaming.

THIRTEEN

Unable to go back to sleep – and not that I would have wanted to anyway – I climbed out of bed, took a quick shower, popped a cold beer, and sat down at my computer to work for a while.

I figured that even if didn't succeed in having her murder solved as a matter of public record, at least folks would have my own record of what happened, to read and make their own decisions on the case.

I could at least keep her *memory* alive.

As I logged in to check my email account, I could see that Wagner had already contacted me, and I wasn't sure if that was good news or bad, considering I had just spoken with him yesterday.

Almost hesitantly, I opened the email to read this:

Mr Polanski

I hate to be the bearer of bad news, but I have been told by my superiors, that I am to immediately terminate my current investigation into the information you provided me with yesterday, and you have been advised to do the same.

My superiors believe that an active investiagtion into a forty year old murder case would be a waste of time at best, since the cause of death was listed as "undetermined."

Once again, I'm very sorry I couldn't help you

My heart dropped in my chest, and I just sat there for the longest time, staring at the computer screen like it was a portal into another dimension.

It may as well have been.

A portal into a world where I, Chuck Polanksi, have proved to be a complete failure once again.

Imagine that.

#

As the day went on, I'd felt more like a complete failure than I ever had before.

I had been a drunk, a jailbird. I'd been a worthless bum with dellusions of grandeur.

I'd been almost everything negative in my life, but I'd never been a real success at anything worth while.

Was this all I was meant to be? A drunken, retired dry cleaning attendant with hopeless dreams of the big time?

No, I thought, stubbornly. *I will NOT be a failure again, no matter what it takes to bring this case to light, like it should have been a long time ago.*

So, I leaned back in my computer chair, took a deep breath, took a drink of my beer, and went back to work on yet another hopeless idea.

Imagine that.

FOURTEEN

A love letter for Loretta.

A constant reminder of a wonderful person who was taken too soon.

If nothing else, I'd leave behind my own version of her legacy, for all of those who loved her to relish and enjoy.

Maybe *that* was my destiny.

I intended to find out soon enough.

But first, my next move in this never ending game of cover up.

It hadn't occurred to me until then, but I could use social media as a weapon. Whereas most folks are using it for gossip and rumor and other nefarious activities, I could use it to shed light on Loretta's case.

So I opened a Facebook group page, in her memory – and, included all I had learned about the case so far, of course.

As I'd expected, all of the local true crime fans had joined the group, and it wasn't long before I had close to one thousand group members, most of them just starving for my next post on the case.

In my experience, your full fledged, dedicated, true cime fans are a totally different *breed* of human being; they seem relatively normal on the outside.

But on the inside, they are craving blood lust and murder and rape and serial killers.

For the next horrifying, blood drenched tale of murder and mayhem.

Just as I had expected, my group page was soon filled with posts and comments on not only Loreatta's case {most of them ridiculous at best} but also their own tall tales of murder and mayhem they'd found on the world wide web, therefore believing they were all true.

After just a few weeks, my group page had turned into a joke.

Just as I'd expected, but deep down had been hoping it wouldn't end up that way.

Once again, the human race had let me down.

But as usual, not for long.

#

Before long, I was back at the helm, with yet another idea to shed light on the case.

I needed a *real* audience.

I needed a press conference.

I needed a *PUBLIC* display of Loretta's case.

So I emailed the local newspaper.

To my surprise, they had replied to my email by the next day.

What shouldn't have been a surprise was, the editor of the paper wasn't interested in my story, or having me interviewed for the paper.

I'd struck out once again.

So, I drank.

FIFTEEN

I drank until my brain felt like it would explode.

I needed to *forget* everything.

At least for the time being, anyway.

It was all I had left that day, my own misery.

My own disappointment.

My own shame.

By the time I'd entered another black out state, I'd finally forgotten about it all.

Until I woke up.

#

A day and a half later, that is.

I woke up on the floor, in front of the couch, with my pants down around my ankles and my shirt stained with puke.

After I'd crawled into the bathroom, managed to stand in front of the mirror, splashing cold water on my face, it was only then had I realized the damage my last black out had caused.

My nose was busted, and caked with blood. I had busted two of my teeth too. I didn't see them lying on the floor, so I guess I had swallowed them.

After downing two beers and a big gulp of single malt, I'd managed to climb in the shower and clean myself up, and slowly but surely made my way to the computer desk.

Where I sat, staring at the screen again, like it was portal into another world.

I had wished it was; anywhere was better than where I was at the time.

I wanted the whole world, just the way I wanted it, and it had let me down again.

But, what really mattered at the time was how well I walked through the fire – without getting burned.

Still, I kept thinking about Loretta. The good parts of our night at the bar felt like a rat walking around and gnawing at the inside of my stomach.

I had to get my shit together fast – and keep it together this time.

Hello, Death. I've had over six decades. I've given you so many clean shots at me, that I should have been yours long ago.

But I'm still here.

So, I carry on.

SIXTEEN

I used to be more sentimental than I am now.

I was sentimental about many things: a woman's shoes under the bed; one hairpin left behind on the dresser; the way they said, 'I'm going to pee.' hair ribbons; walking down the boulevard with them at 1:30 in the afternoon, just two people walking together; the long nights of drinking and smoking; talking; the arguments; thinking of suicide; eating together and feeling good; the jokes; the laughter out of nowhere.

I wonder now, if I may have been thinking about such things the night I was playing pool with Loretta.

She had made me feel *alive* again.

Which, begged the question, was I just infatuated with her, and that's the reason I'm now so hell bent on bringing her killer into the light?

Was it love at first sight, or just infatuation?

Regardless of the reason, here I was again, sitting at my computer, staring at the screen like some kind of nitwit, wishing I was somewhere else.

But where?

That was the question of the day.

#

It didn't take long for me to figure out where I wanted to be – *needed* to be.

Right where I was, sitting at my computer, staring at the screen.

Thinking.

My mind wasn't gone just yet.

The booze hadn't eaten enough brain cells to make me a mental invalid.

What I needed to do, was *open* my mind, to *other* possibilities.

I had spent too much time dwelling on what I could *not* do, instead of what I *could* do, which had been right in front of my face the whole time.

I needed to stay sober – or at least half way sober – long enough to leave my cramped little prison, and go back to the main source of it all, the Third Base bar.

Stop *acting* like an investigator, and start *being* one for a change.

So, that's what I did.

SEVENTEEN

The next day was the first day away from my own little prison, and into the outside world – for more time than it took to walk to the liquor store.

It felt *good*.

I hadn't taken a long walk since I was a teenager. Then again, you have to be sober enough to take a walk before you can do that.

That day, I had decided to be prepared for my walk; two cold beers, a shot of single malt, and a half pint to take on the trip.

After my liquid breakfast, I had set out on my trek, which, if I calculated it correctly, would be around a two mile round trip.

Stepping out into the sunshine, off I went.

#

Back then, I had been living in my first foster home. My first foster family were decent people, but I had rapidly grown tired of spending a lot of my spare time in my tiny little bedroom, staring at the cracks in the ceiling, like they were a roadmap to nowhere.

So, I would take a walkabout.

When most folks hear the word "walkabout," they picture Australia – the land down under – and envision Crocodile Dundee roaming around the bush, saving a damsel in distress from the vicious beasts of the Australian outback.

I'd always enjoyed walking not only for exercise, but because of the things I'd see when I'd walk along at an average pace, taking in all the sights and sounds and the sunlight shining down on me and the breeze blowing through my hair. These are things – the things that a lot of folks consider to be the most small, insignificant things that they sometimes take for granted – that I got to enjoy.

Between bouts of alcoholism, that is.

The sun would just be coming up and the birds would be singing and sometimes a lukewarm breeze would be blowing through my hair as I started out down by the Memorial Bridge and walk the levee out to the local University and stop by the old railroad bridge for a break.

I'd sit there for a while and close my eyes and daydream about the good old days as a kid when my equally worthless friends and I would walk across that bridge on a dare, when we heard a train whistle coming from far away in the distance. We'd wait until the locomotive began crossing the bridge on the Illinois side, barreling down on us with it's horn blaring and smoke spewing and we'd take off toward the Indiana side, hopping off just in time as the train passed by, young and fearless and always tossing caution to the wind.

But today, my primary goal wasn't to revisit the old days; it as to speak to the owner of the Third Base bar, that is, if he was still alive.

#

As it turned out, I had made the trip for nothing.

As I had rounded the corner of Second and St. Clair streets, where the Third Base bar *used* to be, I came face to face with a parking lot.

The whole block had been torn down; the bar, the old IGA foodliner, the houses, *all* of it was *gone*.

As I rounded the corner, I could see that the old Union Tavern about a block away was still standing, so I took a walk up there to see if I could find out anything through small town, drunken gossip.

As it turned out, that was a bust, too.

EIGHTEEN

The bartender at the Union, Lester, an older fella with a receding hairline, John Lennon eyeglasses, and a little pot belly from sampling too much of his own beer, was standing behind the bar when I walked in, reading the morning paper and slurping down some orange juice.

Nearby, two of the tables were occupied by two ladies that had obviously just finished their night shift at the local glass factory, and an older couple, about Lester's age, eating some eggs and bacon and chasing it down with Pabst Blue Ribbon beer.

Some things *never* change.

As I sat down at the bar, Lester looked up from his morning paper and said, "Morning. What can I do for you?"

I said, "I'll take a shot of single malt, straight up."

Glancing around at the not so plentiful selection of liquor bottles on the shelf behind him, he said, "Ain't got no single malt. We got Jack Daniels, Jim Beam, and Calverts. Take your pick."

Debating on it for a moment, I said, "Just give me a draft beer."

After filling a mug and placing it on the bar, he said, "That'll be two bucks."

Fishing my wallet out of my back pocket, I said, "Damn. Last time I bought a draft beer, it was seventy five cents."

Lester just smirked and said, "Inflation, you know?"

I sipped my beer and said, "So, what happened to the bar down the street?"

Lester said, "You mean the Third Base? It was torn down years ago. Where have you been living?"

I grinned and said, "I don't make it out very much these days."

He said, "Apparently not."

I said, "Do you happen to know how I might get ahold of the former owner?"

Lester said, "He died years ago. Why are you asking about him?"

I said, "I'm writing a story about the place. I'm a writer."

Lester said, "Is that so? That's interesting."

I said, "I hope so. But, I need to talk to someone who may or may not have been there back in the seventies. The night that lady was killed."

Lester's facial expression suddenly furrowed into a frown as he said, "Not another one."

I said, "Meaning?"

He said, "A lot of folks have come around asking about that case over the years. Wasting their time, they are. If I was you? I'd just drop the subject and move on to writing about something more interesting, like the local watermelon festival."

I said, adamantly, "I hate watermelon."

Lester said, "Well, you might hate getting your ass kicked a lot more. You need anything else? I'd like to finish reading the paper."

Draining my beer, I said, "You have a good day." Then I stood up and walked out, back to my trek back across town, feeling defeated all over again.

On the way back, I stopped at the railroad bridge, sat down, and lit a cigarette, looking out at the river below, but not day dreaming about my sad youth this time.

I was thinking about Loretta, and *why* nobody wanted to talk about her.

Talk about her *murder.*

I'd heard one time that *small* towns can harbor *big* secrets, and I believed that now. The main question, as always, was *why.*

What was it that she could have said or done to make all of the folks around here want to keep the subject of her death such a big secret?

Forty years later?

It made no sense.

Just like my own pathetic life.

I stood up, popped the cap on my half pint, took a big sip, and raised the bottle in a mock toast and said, "To Loretta."

Then I began the trek back home to receive even more bad news.

#

Upon returning home and turning my computer on, I could see I had a Facebook message from Loretta's daughter, Ann.

I opened it up and began reading the message, hoping for some good news for a change, but I should have known better by now.

As I read it, my heart sank in my chest, a horrible feeling of defeat and helplessness.

Chuck,

> *I know you have put a lot of time and effort into trying to help us, but I don't think I can take any more of this.*

> *It always ends up the same. No matter we find out, it always makes no difference to anyone. And now, my brother, Alan, has found out he has bone cancer, and between my job and helping to take care of him, I barely have time to sleep, let alone take any more disappointments in my mom's case. My mind and heart just can't handle it right now.*

> *Like I said, thank you for your hard work, but I'd really appreciate it if you would just stop writing this story for now.*

> *Sincerely,*
> *Ann*

I just sat there again, staring at the screen like it was a portal into another dimension again. I sat there and sat there and sipped my half pint until it was bone dry, then popped a cold beer.

I drank until I felt like I really *was* in another dimension, and then I poured myself into my bed and closed my eyes, hoping and praying for a goods night's sleep, to forget about all of this madness, if only for a few hours.

But I dreamed instead.

NINETEEN

As I dreamed, my dreams were about Loretta, of course.

In this dream, I was standing in the pool room of the old Third Base bar, listening to the jukebox and boning up on my eight ball, just a few practice shots, when she came walking in the front door.

As she entered the bar, all talking and whispering and music stopped on a dime, as if her very presence there made time stop altogether, and we were all trapped within another dimension.

Some patrons stood frozen in fear, others bolted for the back door.

As I watched her slowly step into the light of the pool room, I could see why the other partons had been so terrified.

When the ghastly thing opened it's mouth, I could have sworn I could smell the overwhelming odor of death itself, coming from deep inside it's decomposing body cavity.

The stomach churning smell of spoiled meat, rotten eggs, and an underlying scent of sickly sweetness that was threatening to make me physically ill.

Then it spoke to me.

WHY HAVEN'T YOU TOLD MY STORY YET?! I NEED YOU TO TELL MY STORY!

I began backing away, tripping over my own feet, and went down hard on my ass, my heart beating right out of my chest.

Then it fell upon me, pinning my arms to the floor, and lowered it's face to my own, it's foul breath choking me.

Then it *kissed* me.

The foul, acrid taste of moldy, earthworm ridden dirt and wilted orchids filled my mouth and throat until I couldn't breathe.

The it leaned over, and whispered to me.

Chuck Polanski, big time writer and worthless drunk. Can't even open his mouth in public unless it's to take a drink. I want to REST IN PEACE!

That's when I woke up, my face bathed in a cold sweat, my whole body trembling.

I glanced around the room, expecting it to jump out of the closet or a corner and finish the job, but nothing happened.

It was just a dream.

Just like my whole miserable life had been; no more than a dream of success and a delusion of grandeur.

I tried to sleep this time, but it never came.

TWENTY

Sitting at the computer, sipping a beer, and staring at the screen again.

No shit shower and shave today; I didn't have the energy.

As I stared at the screen, I had finally realized that there was no other dimension out there; just my own sad reality.

No more pipe dreams, no more dellusions of grandeur.

Just me, and my own sad life.

But it would have to do for now.

#

I had the idea, if I sent my information to the local newspaper, surely the editor would see that *this* time, I had enough good intel to make for a good story. Some front page news.

So, I scanned all of my documents, saved the screen shots, and sent them by email to the editor of the local paper, The Wabash Valley Gazette.

Then, I sat back and *waited*.

No more trips across town, no more phone calls, or in person chats with people who could have cared less.

Just...waiting.

#

Two days went by, then three.

Then a week.

Still no reply email.

Ten days.

Then, finally, a light at the end of the rainbow; a return email from the editor.

I opened it to read this:

To Mr Polanski

I have received your screenshots and document files, and I have carefully looked them over. Although I find the concept of solving this case exciting, I cannot publish them in my newspaper.

As I'd imagine you are already aware of, the cause of the victim's untimely death was listed as an "undetermined cause of death," therefore I cannot publish them as a cold case being solved. If you had more solid information, as well as more people of authority willing to take part in your investigation, I would be more apt to assist you in your current endeavors.

Once again, I apologize for not being able to assist you with this case. I wish you – and the surviving members of her family – the best of luck.

Sincerely,

Lisa Grobbins.

I just sat there staring at the screen again, my heart sinking in my chest and my guts tied up in knots.

I sipped my beer.

Then some single malt.

By the time I was finished that day, I ended up in another black out spell, but this one lasted almost ten years.

Ten years later

TWENTY ONE / May, 2024

I had spent the next ten years in a daze.

One day would melt into another, then to another, and days and weeks and months would go by like a blur.

But I was still alive and kicking.

Barely.

I never forgot about Loretta or her untimely death, either.

#

As the years passed, I had kept in touch with Ann and Gayle, the only other two people who had never given up, either. Ann had given up in a way, but secretly, deep down in her heart, she was still hoping for the best.

Sometimes, all you have left is hope.

I had lost all hope at one point, just watching the days fly by and leave me behind in the dust of the past, yet, I never gave up, either.

Sometimes, hopelessness is all you have left, too.

A deep rooted, pervasive hopelessness that, although depressing and overbearing at times, is still a form of hope, in the way that is always there, reminding you of the main *reason* you feel that way.

Loretta.

Yes, my pretty, petite little blonde, who loved to play pool and listen to the jukebox and drink beer and be sociable.

Until she had been too sociable with the wrong crowd.

The wrong *man*.

Still, no reason to take her life.

The night that Lee had taken her life, he had also taken a lot of other lives with him in the process.

Our hearts. Our minds.

Our very lives.

But, somehow, we moved on.

#

On to *where*, we were still working on that.

In the meantime, as hopeless as it had seemed at the time, I had still been working on the case.

Gayle had been assisting me with it, and Ann had even relented enough to allow me to continue with my story – as long as I didn't post it up on social media, or for sale.

Which was good enough for me; a little progess was better than *no* progress.

In the general scheme of life, you have to take the bad with the good, and do your best to appreciate what you *do* have, and not what you *don't* have.

That, along with some cold beer and single malt, of course.

And my trusty old laptop.

So...we moved on.

#

By the Summer of 2024, not much had changed - in my life, or the lives of others.

The whole world sat by watching helplessly, as our current President, in all of his liberal, Democratic glory, had managed to bring our country to it's knees, and taxing us until we more or less went broke.

In the middle of it all, the American people had nothting better to do at times, than find a way to escape our own sad realities, if only briefly.

Mine was booze, as usual.

Gayle's own escape was babysitting for her grandchildren, and Ann's escape, if you could call it that, was tending to her sister, who had been diagnosed with lung cancer.

Three sad lives, almost intertwined as one, yet seperate.

Three lives searching for something that still wasn't there – but we knew what that something was.

Justice for Loretta.

TWENTY TWO

Public justice, that is.

A loud, almost deafening declaration of justice that been denied to us for too long. The loudest love letter that had ever been written.

I've heard that the best two days in your life, are the day you are born, and the day you realize *why* you were born. By 2024, I had begun to think that I was born to solve this case.

Which I already had, in the long run, but not in the sense of public exposure.

But first, I had to continue with my book.

#

By 2024, the book had laid dormant for too long, and I couldn't wait to get back to work. With Ann and Gayle's permission, I did so, but slowly, as not to make any mistakes along the way.

This time, I concentrated on the ending of the case, and moved backward.

I already knew how it ended; there is one thing for sure.

Upon his death bed, Lee Underhill *admitted* to the killing of Loretta.

He said his conscience was bothering him.

I find it hard to believe he even possessed a

conscience.

I think he was a coward, who was making one last effort not to end up burning in hell – but I doubt if it worked out that way.

Recently, Gayle has told me something interesting; Loretta's husband, Ray, at the time of the murder, suspected Lee Underhill was the one who had killed his wife.

My question is, *why* did he suspect Lee? There had to be a *reason* for his suspicions. Sadly, Ray passed away many years ago, so we can't ask him why he felt that way.

But I'd *love* to know *why.*

#

Why hadn't Lee come forward in those sixteen years years before his death?

Think of the pure Hell Loretta's husband and children had to go through during all of this unnecessary madness.

How could he be a co-worker of Ray's, no less – just stand back and keep his mouth shut while watching Ray and his children suffer for all those years? If you could actually feel any shame or remorse at all, how could you just stand back and watch all of this heartbreaking, horrible madness unfold without saying anything?

The answer is simple enough.

You have absolutely *NO* conscience whatsoever.

Deep down, you are nothing more than a cold hearted, self centered *monster,* whose idea of having a "good time" is taking advantage of unsuspecting victims who are easy targets – and, if the victim refuses their advances?

They pay for it with their very life.

Just like Loretta paid for it with her own life, on September 7th, 1974.

TWENTY THREE

Onward we go again – backward – so pay attention.

After a long day, Loretta decides to walk down to the local tavern, Burke's, {later known as The Third Base, not to be confused with the Imperial tavern} for drinks and friendly banter with some of the other bar patrons. It's just like any other September night, a typical Indiana twilight, clear, perfect, and breezy.

As you walk along, enjoying the weather on your way to see your friends, you can smell pizza and hot-dogs in the air, and hear the sounds of neighborhood children playing nearby and the steady but quiet hum of traffic as it glides along Second Street, more hard working folks on their way home to eat dinner, shower, and then out to congregate with friends and family.

This is *her* world: nothing fancy, but very important and endearing to her nonetheless.

As Loretta walks into the bar, all who know her turn to greet her with big smiles and friendly hugs, always glad to see her and feeling all the more blessed to be in her presence. Over the next few hours, friendly banter is exchanged, beer mugs are refilled, jokes are told and the music blaring from the ancient jukebox helps set the mood for the rest of the evening. Everyone knows everyone else here, and the overall mood is normally one of fun and celebration for the simple things in life, a festive atmosphere – unless a fight breaks out now and then, over a girlfriend or a pool game. Typical small town bar on a weekend.

Then, at the end of the evening, apparently oblivious to everyone else, Loretta simply *vanishes*, and right under everyone's nose, in a terrifying turn of events that would last for an excruciating six weeks before her family and friends learned of her fate.

One local man, Lee Underhill, were there that night, too – and seemed to simply vanish into thin air, too, but possibly in the company of Loretta.

But, nobody saw or heard anything?

That's bullshit.

#

Mankind's cruelty knows no bounds.

German philosopher Friedrich Nietzsche once said, "mankind is the cruelest animal," and I tend to agree with him.

Who else but a cold, cruel, calculated, remorseless killer would pick a pretty face out of the crowd – and a familiar face, no less – and, after being refused his intentions toward her, would beat and choke her to death, and dump her lifeless body in a cornfield like trash?

The *who* has been answered now, but the *why* may always remain a mystery.

TWENTY FOUR

I have just been informed that my neighbor, the lady I spoke with so many years ago, has now agreed to hold court with Ann and Gayle again, so maybe the *why* Lee did it may come to light, too.

But I doubt it.

Besides, I'd hate to think that someone who lives right down the alley from me would have kept things a secret this long, too. That in itself made me feel kinda creepy, you know?

So, as I wait for what may or not be good news, I pop a nice cold beer. Like I said before, some things *never* change.

But I honestly wouldn't have had it any other way.

Not that I actually *enjoy* being miserable, mind you, but at times, in the past, it has made me a stronger and more determined man.

One thing I've learned along the way, though; I *can* actually feel lonely.

Human relationships were strange. I mean, you were with one person a while, eating and sleeping and living with them, loving them, talking to them, going places together, and then it stopped.

Then there was a short period when you weren't with anybody, then another woman arrived, and you ate with her and drank with her, and it all seemed so normal, as if you had been waiting just for her and she had been waiting for you. I never felt right being alone; sometimes it felt good but it never felt right.

Just like it had with Loretta, after looking back on that night.

We had drank and laughed and played pool and had a good time, that is for two total strangers. After what happened to her, I had felt such a sense of loss and loneliness.

Sometimes, unfortunately for guys like me, loneliness is your only friend.

But, as usual, I manage to move on.

#

I still think that I'm just an alcoholic who became a writer so that I would be able to stay in bed until noon, but at least now I can admit it to myself.

That's another thing I can thank Loretta for; her death made me open my eyes to who and what I really was – and it has served me well – most of the time, anyway.

Just like today.

As I sit at my computer, typing away, and waiting for Ann or Gayle to hopefully relay some good news, I don't feel lonely anymore.

That's because I am doing something worthwhile, instead of just being a lonely, drunken mess of a man.

So I move on.

TWENTY FIVE

Once again, I moved on to more bad news.

As it turned out, Ann and Gayle's conversations with Lee's granddaughter didn't really amount to much, other than what she'd already told us – or we'd figured out on our own already.

But, it was *something*, and it was more than we'd had before this all began.

We couldn't look a gift horse in the mouth, so to speak.

So we moved on.

#

Weeks dragged by, and to our surprise, nothing seemed all that different.

I mean, yes, we were so thrilled at having solved the case, but we still didn't feel much different than we had before.

We still felt sad, and still felt as though the case had dragged on too long, while the family served their own life sentence in hell.

Our minds and hearts were worn out, and we would never be the same; that empty void inside, where Loretta used to be, would never be filled again – unless it was with simple memories and brief flashbacks of long ago.

But, we thought that was much better than nothing.

Yes, we lost a special person to us all.

Yes, that void will always be there.

But we are all still here, carrying on her legacy, and keeping her memory alive.

That's what *really* matters.

#

It's been a long, hard road.

But we made it.

As I sit at my computer today – sober, this time – for the first time in months, I feel like celebrating *without* alcohol.

That, in itself, is a victory.

Just like our other small but very significant victories, that seem so small but mean so much.

Sometimes, it's the small, hard earned victories that are most important to us, and our well being.

To our heart and soul.

I'm sure that somewhere, high above our heads beyond the clouds and the stars, in a better place, Loretta is happy now too, finally at peace, not only proud of us for sticking through it all, but also because someone *loved* her enough to make sure she got the justice she deserved.

God bless you, dear lady, we miss you.

I hope you enjoyed your love letter, too.

Afterword

In September of 1974, a local Vincennes woman, Dolores Oliver, seemed to vanish without a trace.

Weeks later, her body was found in a corn field in Illinois.

For the next 47 years, the case went unsolved.

Fifty years later, in 2024, due to a local resident reading my first book on the case, and coming forward with some valuable information, the case has been solved; her own grandfather, who was a rapist and pedophile, had admitted to the murder in a death bed confession.

A Love Letter To Loretta is just that; a declaration of love and devotion and determination against all odds to bring her killer into the light, after so many years of the truth being shrouded in darkness.

#

The character of Chuck Polanksi was based on me, and my years as an alcoholic. I have now been sober for seventeen years.

The character of Loretta of course, is based on Mrs Dolores Oliver, who was murdered on September 7th, 1974.

Lee Underhill Jr is based on a real man, the man responsible for the death of Dolores Oliver.

Unfortunately, he died many year ago, so he can't be prosecuted for her death. But, now we *KNOW* who committed the crime.

Most importantly, case has been *solved*.

Case photos:

Lee Underhill, wearing a big smile for the camera, the image hiding his real self; a cold hearted killer.

North Second Street in Vincennes, Indiana, in the early 70s. Not too far down this street, on September 7th, 1974, Lee Underhill picked Dolores up and took her for what would be a the last ride of her life.

News clippings of Underhill's arrest and conviction for child molestation.

Junior L Underhill. 55. was being held early today at the jail on $3,000 bond. According to court records, Underhill is charged with molesting a 12-year-old girl on April 1 Arraignment is set for 8 45 a.m Friday in Superior Court.

State vs. Junior Lee Underhill, 55, Evansville.

Underhill pleaded guilty to a charge of molesting a five-year-old girl. He was ordered to the Department of Correction's Reception and Diagnostic Center, Plainville, for evaluation. He will be sentenced after the evaluation and a pre-sentence investigation by the Knox County Probation Department.

The incident occurred on July 5 and charges were filed on July 16.

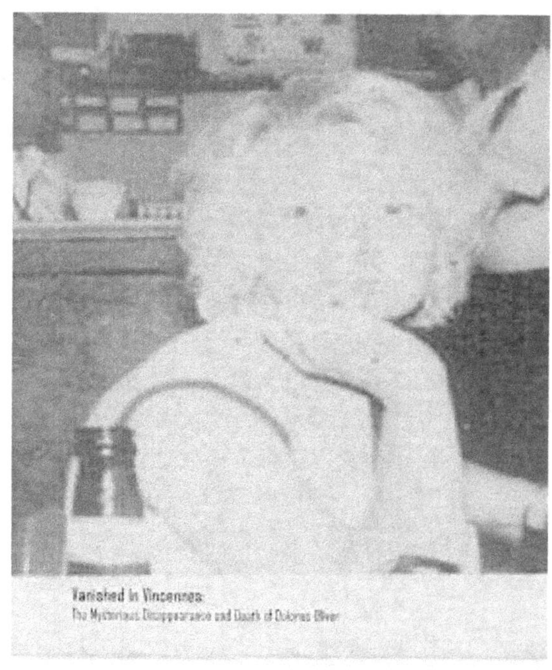

Dolores Oliver, known fondly to her friends as "Lert," at the local tavern with her friends.

Little did she know that her life would soon end in such a tragic way, and at the hands of a man she thought she could trust.

Two of the original autopsy documents, which you can see have water damage due to a leak in the roof of the evidence room of the Lawrenceville Illinois PD.

These are also some of the evidence that now have mysteriously disappeared.

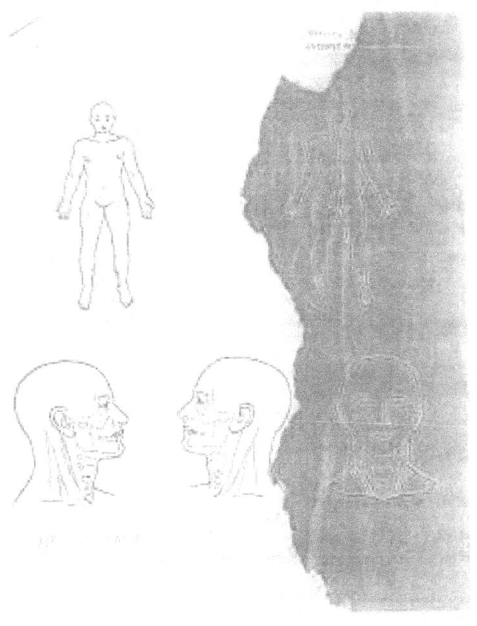

AUTOPSY SUMMATION

David Boyer is a Christian, a multi-genre writer, a true crime buff, and the author of several coming of age novellas, numerous horror and scifi stories, as well as the author of numerous essays including the subjects of government corruption, Christianity, bullying, and cyber-stalking.

He lives in Vincennes, Indiana, with his cat, Holly Jean, who now serves as his copy editor by jumping on the computer keyboard when he's not looking.

Books: {Non-fiction}
True crime:
Small Town Murder: True Crime Stories From Knox County, Indiana
Murder In the Hoosier Heartland: Infamous Indiana Murderers & Fledgling Serial Killers
Murder & Mayhem In the Hoosier Heartland: Mysterious Disappearances & Bizarre Murders In Indiana
The Blitz: A Rape Victim's Story
Vanished In Vincennes: the Mysterious Disappearance and Death Of Dolores Oliver
47 Years of Hell: The Dolores Oliver Murder: Still Unsolved
Small Town Murder In Knox County, Indiana: Hate Crimes, Witch Hunts, and A Definitive List of Indiana Serial Killers
The Guy In The Blue Shirt

Non-fiction: {paranormal, bio & memoir}
Haunted Heartland: Haunted Hoosiers Tell Their Ghost Stories
Strange Happenings In the Hoosier Heartland
I Remember When, In Vincennes...Volume 1
Growing Up In Vincennes – Volumes 2 – 5
The Time of Our Lives: Growing Up Cool In Vincennes, Indiana

Essays:
Bullying: the Road to Recovery and Forgiveness
Privacy In the Age of the Internet: How Sexting and Sharing Private Photos Can lead To Cyber-Stalking
Once An Alcoholic, Always An Alcoholic? The Cold Hard Truth

About Our Addictions
Travesties of Jutice: Flaws In Our Legal System That Imprison the Innocent
Will the REAL Christian Please Stand Up?
Racism in the 21ˢᵗ Century: ALL Lives Matter
Conflicted Souls: How the Man In Black Saved My Life
Crossing the Rainbow Bridge: Saying Goodbye To Our Beloved Pets

Books: {Fiction}
Mystery, Indiana
Human Sawdust

Stories: {Long fiction, novellas}
Mystery, Indiana
The Mind of Luther Biggs
LUTHER
Jenny
Lester Talbot and His Magic Eye
Beautiful Ghosts
Pretty Flamingo
Jack and Norma Jean
The Things We Leave Behind – Volumes 1 – 3
Ghosts of Summer
Gardens
Claustrophobia
The Cemetery Artist
Brain Pie
Beast
The Jailhouse Movie Star
Easy Pickings
The Dominant Thumb
Joyride
The Maverick
Freak
Grandma's Gooseberry Pie
Dancing With the King
Always In My Heart

Hillbilly Moonshine Zombies
Home
Sheva
A Debt Repaid In Full
The Enlightening Darkness
The Good Neighbor
Wander
The Hungry Ones
A Gunfighter's Legacy
Dead Man's Hand
Inhuman Experiments – Part 1, 2, and 3
Jennifer
Spider Bait
Goodnight, My Love
Poor Larry
Creepy Crawl
The Ballad Of Georgie

Dolores Oliver, fondly nick-named 'Lert' by her friends as a term of endearment, was out an out-going and friendly woman who was well liked by all who knew her.

Yet, on September 7, 1974, while on a visit to a local bar to chat with friends, she simply vanished without a trace. Foul play was immediately suspected by her family, who knew in their hearts that they could think of absolutely no one who would want to do her any harm.

Yet her lifeless body was found at the end of October in a bean field by a farmer in Illinois. Lawrence County coroner Dale Nichols was able to make a positive ID through dental records and a ring Mrs Oliver was wearing.

Who would have done such a thing, and why? Hopefully, VANISHED IN VINCENNES will help to finally solve one of the oldest cold cases in Indiana, and bring her family some closure they have sought for so long.

I Remember When, In Vincennes...

Hometown Stories From
Vincennes, Indiana - Volume 1

David Boyer

Unfortunately, even small towns – Vincennes included – eventually change, sometimes for the better, and other times, not so much. It's the natural order of things.

Trees grow old and fall. Sidewalks split and crack and are replaced for public safety's sake. Old houses – and all the memories associated with them – are demolished and replaced with parking lots or duplexes. Even historical landmarks, Mother Nature and Father Time having taken their toll, sadly, vanish – except for our own pictures and memories of them.

Luckily for Vincennes residents, local historian Norbert Brown has created a Facebook group page entitled, *Vincennes Remember When*, to help all of us keep our fond memories intact, and to reminisce and enjoy them 24-7.

It was his infinite wisdom of our local history and group page that was the inspiration for this book – and the stories within. Some of these stories may elicit a tear, some laughter.

Some may remind you of an old friend you haven't seen since high school – or, sadly, one that has passed in recent years. Some may remind you of your childhood, your teenage years – or having to bid them farewell, in order to move on to bigger and better things; marriage, children, grandchildren, and a lifetime of wonderful memories that only a tight-knit, loving family can provide.

It is my sincere belief that there will be a story for *everybody* within these pages, regardless of whether you may be a Vincennes history buff or not.

As of 2015, it is believed that there are at least 200 serial killers active in the United States at any given time.

33 of them were from Indiana.

Nobody in their own home town would have wanted to imagine a fledgling {or full fledged} serial killer lurking about, searching for his next victim. Or imagine one being their next door neighbor or the relative of a friend or even attending the local college.

Yet, since the early 1970s, Vincennes, Indiana, Knox County, and Indiana in general has had it's share of cold blooded murder.

It's really sad – as well as terrifying – to even imagine all these brutal, cold blooded murders have taken place in small town communities, where, at one time, we could all trust just about everyone we met at least to the extent they'd do us no harm; a time when could leave our doors unlocked at night or a window open for a cool breeze or not have to worry about where our children were – or if they'd ever come home again.

In SMALL TOWN MURDER, we will be examining local cases, old cases, more recent cases, and the aftermath it leaves behind for the victim's families – as well as taking an in-depth look into a deep, dark, world none of us would ever want to see – but has been here all along, and, most likely, always will be.

Bonus:
Excerpts from the book
Vanished In Vincennes
The Mysterious Disappearance and Death of Dolores Oliver
By David Boyer

For Dolores:
Still loved and sadly missed by family and friends.

Introduction:

The Northern side of Vincennes, known infamously as "the North end," in the 1970s, was, at one point, a melting pot of crime.

Drugs, alcohol, burglary, arson, street fighting, and bar brawling was the norm on any given day. Residents were in fear of their safety after dark – and at times even during the daytime hours. In the North end you either belonged or you didn't and if you didn't, you didn't come in less you got your ass whipped.

Street toughs ruled their corner of the block, and dared any "outsider" to cross their turf. A trip to the store for a loaf of bread was considered an act of bravery. But regardless of the area's well deserved reputation, there were families that lived within the community, that, regardless of their so called "tough reputation," were in reality no more dangerous than we would consider ourselves to be.

So was the Oliver family. Raymond Oliver was a hard working man doing his best to provide for his wife and seven children in a tough part of town, which made it even harder to do so, with all the temptations of local crime and the party lifestyle so available to his kids.

Yet he persevered. His wife, Dolores, fondly nick-named 'Lert' by her friends as a term of endearment, was out an out-going and friendly woman who was well liked by all who knew her.

Yet, on September 7, 1974, while on a visit to a

local bar to chat with friends, she simply vanished without a trace. Foul play was immediately suspected by her family, who knew in their hearts that they could think of absolutely no one who would want to do her any harm.

Yet her lifeless body was found at the end of October in a bean field by a farmer in Illinois. Lawrence County coroner Dale Nichols was able to make a positive ID through dental records and a ring Mrs Oliver was wearing.

Vincennes Detective Leslie Chanley was assigned to the case, and that had seemed to be when the case went sour – and came to a complete standstill.

It is my hope that the information in this chapbook, examined from a point of view other than law enforcement and social media, will shed some light on the circumstances surrounding the case.

Radio personality Paul Harvey once said, "If you want to get away with murder? Just go to Vincennes, Indiana." Sadly, in September of 1974, that comment rang true.

David Boyer / August, 2018

To have even a basic understanding of what may or may not have happened, let us establish a "time line," so to speak:

September 7, 1974 – early evening.

After a long day, Mrs Oliver decides to walk down to the local tavern, Burke's, {later known as The Third Base, not to be confused with the Imperial tavern} for drinks and friendly banter with some of the other bar patrons. It's just like any other September night, a typical Indiana twilight, clear, perfect, and breezy. As you walk along, enjoying the weather on your way to see your friends, you can smell pizza and hot-dogs in the air, and hear the sounds of neighborhood children playing nearby and the steady but quiet hum of traffic as it glides along Second Street, more hard working folks on their way home to eat dinner, shower, and then out to congregate with friends and family. This is *her* world: nothing fancy, but very important and endearing to her nonetheless.

As Mrs Oliver walks into the bar, all who know her turn to greet her with big smiles and friendly hugs, always glad to see her and feeling all the more blessed to be in her presence. Over the next few hours, friendly banter is exchanged, beer mugs are refilled, jokes are told and the music blaring from the ancient jukebox helps set the mood for the rest of the evening. Everyone knows everyone else here, and the overall mood is normally one of fun and celebration for the simple things in life, a festive atmosphere – unless a fight breaks out now and then, over a girlfriend or a pool game. Typical small town bar on a weekend. Then, at the end of the evening, apparently oblivious to everyone else, Mrs Dolores Oliver simply *vanishes*, and right under everyone's nose, in a terrifying turn of events that would last for an excruciating six weeks before her family and friends learned of her fate.

Over the next six, long, excruciating weeks, her family and friends could only sit back and wonder: Why didn't *anyone* see her leave the bar? And if so, why didn't they step forward with any crucial information, such as a description of the potential suspect? For some reason, the place where she had always felt safe was now full of people keeping their mouths shut and turning a blind eye to the recent disappearance of a beloved friend.

The nightmarish visions that went through their minds I am sure was a torturous punishment no family should have to endure. Where could she be? She wouldn't just take off with a friend or go out drinking and not contact her family. It was rumored that at times, if she and her husband were not getting along, she would leave for a couple of days, but she would always come back unscathed. Otherwise, she was known to be a very good hearted woman, too, who would do almost anything to help a person in need. If you were hungry? She would gladly make you something to eat. Needed a place to stay? No problem, there's the couch.

It didn't take them long to realize and face up to the fact that foul play most definitely had to be involved.

But...*who* would want to hurt her? And *why?*

Yet, someone must have had what they *thought* was a reason to harm her. Her niece, Gaye Collins Dillon, told me the following heartbreaking story after visiting the murder site:

I remember going over to the cornfield you could see the outline of her body, pieces of her hair was in the mud, her finger nails where laying there , little pieces of her skirt was in the mud. She had laid there in muddy water for a while and they said the animals and the birds had got to her. It was horrible. Was she killed here and then dumped over there? WHY wasn't anyone trying to help us find out what happened?

Very good question.

Rayetta Mincey, Mrs Oliver's eldest daughter, had this to say:

When Mom first went missing, my dad and my brothers went everywhere to look for her , if any one thought they saw her. it didn't matter where, they would go, this went on the entire time she was missing. It was always a big let down when they would return from a sighting and didn't have any news, We always felt like the police were not doing anything and we all felt helpless.The not knowing was so hard, always wondering if she was hurt some where and couldn't get help or if she was being held against her will, the thoughts you have are horrible. None of us really knew what to do. But we all KNEW something was wrong.

Something was wrong, indeed.

Something *horribly* wrong.

Who else but her own, close-knit family would *know* that there had to be foul play involved? Why were their pleas for help or information ignored? Why wasn't her case given more consideration?

This is what her family had to endure for over six weeks - and beyond - without any results excepting for her ghastly, untimely death.

October 25th, 1974 – to present day.

There are many theories that have surrounded this case, one of which, I am sure, is that Mrs Oliver just simply ran away from home with another man, to escape the responsibility of her own home life, and her new boyfriend just happened to turn out to be a killer. Another was that her husband was angry with her for something, and he did it in a fit of rage. {This is also very doubtful, because Raymond Oliver was known to have loved his wife very much, and never remarried after her death.}

In yet another, it was rumored that someone she knew from Illinois did it, {hence the body dump in Illinois} but that theory has never been proven either. In small town murder cases, rumors and gossip usually abound to no end, and now, with social networking web sites like Facebook available for gossip mongers to post their BS and drama, it's even worse.

I, myself, have already dismissed this theory under the circumstances, after corresponding with her family. I realize that the police must always examine a murder case from all angles, in order to eliminate innocent people from the suspect list, but in this case, I just found it to be totally absurd.

Another theory the police always consider is that a murder victim could have been preyed upon by a drifter just passing through. In my own personal studies of serial killers, I have noticed that a lot of them are *drifters*, who live a nomadic lifestyle, who kill and then move on quickly, in order to elude capture. Some even change there MO as well, shooting one victim, stabbing another, to throw the police off their trail and confuse them. Serial killer Henry Lee Lucas was known to have passed through Indiana in the early 70s upon his release from prison, too, but I have dismissed this theory because the timeline between her death and his release just didn't add up.

But with this case, I have my sincere doubts about the aforementioned theories, and have come up with my own.

I, myself, believe that it was someone who knew her *personally*, if only in passing, maybe a so called "friendly acquaintance," someone she would not suspect of any wrong doing, would have no motive to harm her, and that is how they got away with her murder. Someone she had a beer with now and then. Just another harmless, friendly face in the crowd.

Until just the right moment, when that friendly face suddenly turned into a mask of horror and malice, and it was too late to turn back.

I may be wrong, but I don't think so.